Real Dogs Don't Eat Leftovers

AUTHOR'S NOTE

This book is printed on recycled paper. After all, where would Real Dogs be if we cut down all the trees?

AUTHOR'S NOTE

Real Dogs Don't Eat Leftovers

Written and Illustrated by Lee Lorenz

LONG SHADOW BOOKS
PUBLISHED BY POCKET BOOKS NEW YORK

This book is gratefully dedicated to that peerless chronicler of Real Men, Bruce Feirstein. Without his original, brilliant conception it could never have been produced.

Special thanks also to Marty Asher, Trish Todd, and Jacques Chazaud who knocked the whole thing into shape.

An *Original* publication of LONG SHADOW BOOKS

A Long Shadow Book published by
POCKET BOOKS, a division of Simon & Schuster, Inc.
1230 Avenue of the Americas, New York, N.Y. 10020

ISBN: 0-671-47757-9

First Long Shadow Books printing September, 1983

10 9 8 7 6 5 4 3 2 1

LONG SHADOW and colophon are trademarks
of Simon & Schuster, Inc.

Printed in the U.S.A.

Design by Jacques Chazaud

Contents

1. Introduction 11

2. The Real Dog's Credo 12

3. Today's Real Dog 13

Real Dog Quiz #1 17

4. The Origin of Real Dogs 19

Real Dog Quiz #2 21

5. Real Dogs Through the Ages 22

Real Dog Quiz #3 31

6. Great Dates and Black Dates in Real Dog History 32

7. The Real Dog Test 34

8. Real Dogs of Famous People 35

9. Naming the Real Dog **45**

10. Sex and the Real Dog **47**

11. The Real Dog Library **49**

12. How to Be Your Own
Best Friend's Best Friend **50**

13. Real Dog Humor **53**

14. Is Your Dog Real?
Seven Danger Signals and
What to Do About Them **64**

15. The Real Dog Hit Parade **67**

16. Living with the Real Dog **68**

17. Dog House—Right **70**

18. Dog House—Wrong **71**

19. Five Things You Won't Find
in a Real Dog's Stomach **72**

Real Dog Quiz #4 **73**

20. The Real Dog's Wardrobe   *74*

Real Dog Quiz #5   *76*

21. Portraits of Real Dogs by Famous Artists   *77*

22. Great Real Dog Quotes   *88*

23. The Real Dog Hall of Fame   *89*

Real Dog Quiz #6   *93*

24. A Final Word   *94*

1

Introduction

Thanks to Bruce Feirstein and Joyce Jillson we now know all there is to know about Real Men and Real Women. But haven't we left something out? Who helped the first Real Man track down the first bison burger? Who stood guard while the first Real Woman put on her makeup? The first Real Dog, of course.

In the following pages we celebrate this remarkable creature. We examine his humble beginnings, his triumphs, and, yes, his tragedies. Most importantly, we discuss his increasingly precarious position in today's confusing world, and offer some suggestions for dealing with it.

For just as Real Men are finding their favorite bars full of quiche-eaters, Real Dogs find themselves surrounded by boot-licking, Perrier-drinking, lap-warming imitations.

We hope this book will serve as both a call to arms and a battle plan for Real Dogs everywhere. We owe them that much.

Without Real Dogs, man would never have invented the wheel, discovered fire, or developed home video recorders. And Real Women would still be pounding clothes on rocks, while waiting for the first issue of *Cosmopolitan*.

2

The Real Dog's Credo

Anything worth eating in a doggie bag
is not for the dog.

3

---

*Today's
Real Dog*

his was it.

Exit 12 off Interstate 114 just south of Scranton.

I swung down the ramp and into the parking lot of Big Red's Pit Stop.

It was 3:30 A.M. and the lot was almost empty. I parked next to a sixteen-wheel rig covered with warning signs—Danger: Nuclear Waste. I noticed the Pass, No-Pass signs on its rump:

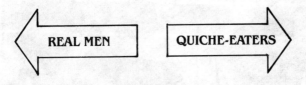

My man was already there.

As I entered, the bartender was dusting off the hard-boiled eggs. He silently motioned me toward the booths in the rear. I slogged through the butts and sawdust to the last one.

"Flex Crush?" I asked, extending my hand.

"The same," he replied, taking my fingers in a grip that made my ears pop.

"Meet Nuke," he said, indicating the hulking shape seated next to him.

"Duke?"

"Nuke—as in 'Nuke 'Em.' "

"Er—good to meet you, Nuke."

I held out my still throbbing hand. In response, Nuke blinked his eyes and slowly curled back his upper lip, exposing a row of large, very sharp teeth.

Flex drained his bottle of Iron City beer. "Real Dogs don't shake," he said.

I had been anticipating this meeting for weeks, and obviously I was off on the wrong foot.

"Is Nuke your dog?" I asked, attempting to regain my composure.

Flex thought for a moment.

"Nuke belongs to me the way I belong to the VFW— by choice. Real Dogs don't really *belong* to anybody. I guess you could say we hang out together."

The waiter arrived with two bottles of beer. I looked inquiringly at Nuke.

"Nuke's on duty in a hour," said Flex. "Security at a toxic waste facility. He never drinks when he's working." He turned to the waiter. "Double burgers all around, heavy on the onions."

The waiter shuffled off.

Flex hunched forward.

"So you want to know about Real Dogs. What can I tell you? When I was a kid that's the only kind there was. Everybody had one. Hamsters were still doing medical research and gerbils hadn't been invented. Real Dogs were a Real Kid's best friend. Nowadays everyone's supposed to be their *own* best friend. No wonder Real Dogs are suffering from identity crises. Back then no one would have confused a Real Dog with the drooling, cuddly, simpy, wimpy, lap-warmers you see around today."

The burgers arrived, and while Flex anointed them with chili sauce, I took a good look at Nuke. He had short hair, broad shoulders, a long snout, and pointed ears. He was an indeterminate color—not black or brown, just dark. He wore a thick leather collar with studs. His front paws were on the table and his nails were unclipped. He caught me looking at him and returned my gaze with an intensity that made me turn away.

"So how does one recognize a Real Dog?" I asked.

"Real Dogs don't have three names.

"Real Dogs don't eat anything that makes its own gravy.

"Real Dogs don't wear rhinestone collars, rain hats, or rubber boots.

"They are not offended by doggie odors.

"They never 'have' papers, although they might deign to carry them.

"Real Dogs are not sanitized, deodorized, personalized or accessorized.

"Real Dogs are self-confident enough to be cooperative but independent enough to be interesting. In short, a Real Dog is everything a Real Man needs that he can't find anywhere else. Loyalty, discretion, and comradeship, without this smarmy togetherness."

Flex paused and checked his battered Timex.

"Gotta roll," he said, hoisting himself out of the booth.

I was so absorbed in Flex's conversation that I had hardly touched my burger. In a last effort to ingratiate myself with Nuke I slid it toward him. With a low growl he slid it back.

Crush zipped up his Windbreaker and lit a Camel.

He blew a perfect smoke ring and smiled a crooked smile.

"Real Dogs," he said, "don't eat leftovers."

Real Dog
Quiz #1

Q. Admiral Byrd was actually the ninth one to reach the South Pole. Who were the first eight?

A. His sled dogs.

4

*The Origin of
Real Dogs*

Where do Real Dogs come from?

The creationist maintains they, like everything else, sprang full-blown from the brow of the Almighty twelve thousand years ago. The evolutionist suggests a more leisurely descent from some feral wolflike ancestor. (We can ignore those weenies who think they came from places like Paws and Claws and Pets 'R' Us.)

Real Dogs themselves trace their lineage back to the Garden of Eden. Some feel the first dog left with Adam and Eve out of sheer boredom. Others maintain they were banished for committing the first public nuisance in the otherwise unblemished paradise.

Whatever the case, it's clear that dogs have been man's companion, helpmeet, and friend since earliest times. Obviously, such a durable relationship is not casual and bespeaks a deep mutuality of interest.

Real Dogs chose men as men chose Real Dogs.

To the ancient question, If he follows you home can you keep him? the answer is: only if he wants to stay.

The Evolution of Real Dogs and Real Men

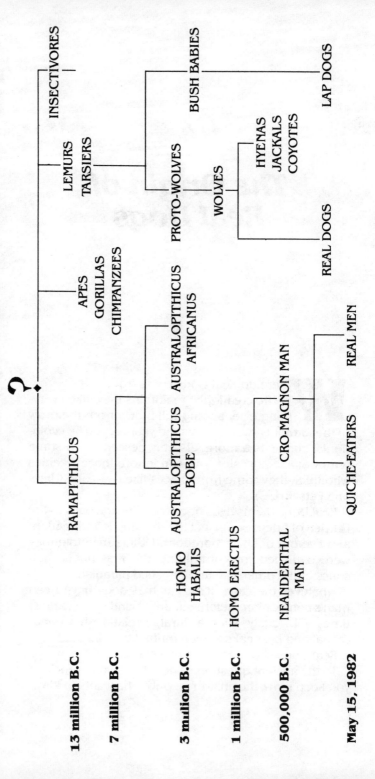

13 million B.C.

7 million B.C.

3 million B.C.

1 million B.C.

500,000 B.C.

May 15, 1982

Real Dog
Quiz #2

Q. What kind of salutation does a Real
Dog put on his Father's Day card?

A. To whom it may concern.

5

*Real Dogs
Through the Ages*

A hundred thousand years ago, Neanderthal man was the only game in town. He was not exactly stimulating company, but early dogs found him to be a steady and dependable master. Then some fifty thousand years later, a more entertaining, more intelligent variation appeared—Cro-Magnon man. Real Dogs immediately sensed his potential, and Neanderthals were left to shift for themselves. In despair, they attempted to domesticate cats. Shortly afterward, they disappeared altogether. (Serves them right.)

Cro-Magnon man and early dogs were a hot team, and before you could say *Australoplithicus Africanus* they were grilling reindeer steaks over something called fire. They moved into caves and invented interior decoration.

Real Dogs, however, are restless and adventuresome by nature, and eventually they moved on to search the European continent for a more well-rounded diet.

In 5000 B.C. Real Dogs were in Britain when the rising sea cut it off from the mainland. With typical Real Dog patience, they hunkered down and waited for mutton to be invented.

REAL DOGS DISCOVER FIRE
50,000 B.C.

Good work, gentlemen. I'm sure the gods are very pleased.

Early Civilization

The importance of Real Dogs to men grew so rapidly that by the time the first civilizations were forming, the dog had become man's indispensable companion. Dog worship was almost universal. *All* the earliest ceremonial centers, from the Mayans in Mexico to the Pyramids of Egypt, are oriented to the dog star, Sirius. This is also true of Stonehenge, the giant statues on Easter Island, and the mysterious lines on the Nazca Plains in Peru. And it surely is no coincidence that the first day of the Egyptian calendar, which begins in 4236 B.C., is May 12, Rin-Tin-Tin's birthday!

Perhaps the most monumental reminder of dog worship is the great sphinx, erected in Giza in 2550 B.C. It was modeled after the sacred dog of the sun king Amenhotep. (Some people have actually suggested that the sphinx is supposed to be a cat. Ridiculous. Did you ever see a cat sitting like that?)

A few other important dates in early history:

8000 B.C. Agriculture is discovered. Civilization changes from a hunting-gathering society to a settled, agricultural one. Real Dogs take up sheep-herding.

7000 B.C. Metal-working is developed. First Real Dog collar is forged.

2000 B.C. Shang Dynasty rises in China. Silk industry makes it wealthy and powerful. Roast dog becomes a delicacy.

1960 B.C. Real Dogs leave China in disgust, and civilization collapses.

The Classical Period

With the rise of the rational spirit in Greece, dog worship began to fade. Yet even there, the importance of dogs as a symbol never waned. The legend of the

founding of Rome involves twins, Romulus and Remus. At birth, they were abandoned in the plains and
might have died if they had not been found and
suckled by a she-dog (sometimes mistranslated as
she-wolf). They survived and founded Rome. Subse-
quently they quarreled over the question of which one
Mommy loved best, and Romulus killed Remus. (Or
Remus killed Romulus. No one was ever sure which.)

The Dark Ages

After the collapse of the Roman Empire, Europe
sank into barbarism and despair. Mankind might have
disappeared altogether if Real Dogs hadn't helped out
by gathering sticks for firewood and keeping people
from bumping into each other in the dark. (The ances-
tors of seeing-eye dogs first appeared during this
period.)

The Middle Ages and the Renaissance

During the Middle Ages, the torch of civilization
burned low, and Real Dogs fell in man's esteem.
Indeed, they became scapegoats for some of history's
greatest tragedies. The Great Plague of 1347–51 was
spread by fleas, and Real Dogs were widely held
responsible and run out of town.

The Hundred Years War followed (1338–1453),
proving that without Real Dogs man had now lost even
the ability to count.

Then things got even worse. The achievements of
the classical past were rediscovered and a great burst
of intellectual energy launched what we now call the
Renaissance. It was a man-centered society.
Leonardo, for example, considered man the measure
of all things. Gone were the days when man re-
sponded so readily to the Real Dogs's gentle teaching,

THE DARK AGES AND THE
ORIGINS OF THE SEEING EYE DOG

NEWLY DISCOVERED PAGE FROM
LEONARDO'S 'MIRROR' NOTEBOOKS

loyalty, and good nature. The deeper values Real Dogs had taught their masters were pushed aside in man's search for novelty and sensationalism.

In 1457 movable type made possible the wide dissemination of reading material. At this point the first No Dogs Allowed signs were printed.

But Real Dogs knew their unerring patience would be rewarded and that men would become good masters once again. In 1492, it was Columbus's dogs Nina, Pinta, and Santa Maria who drew his attention to the shape of the moon. From this he deduced that the earth was also round, and the age of discovery began. In recognition of Real Dogs' contribution to this new spirit of adventure, Lorenzo de Medici commissioned Benvenuto Cellini to design and execute the first (and only) solid silver dog house (now in the Vatican Library). In 1606 Shakespeare wrote *Macbeth* and the first great dog one-liner entered the English language: "Out, out, damned spot!"

By the seventeenth century, man was crossing the oceans as easily as he once crossed the Danube.

In 1620 the Pilgrims landed at Plymouth Rock and soon afterward the first puppy was born in the New World.

The challenge of this new country bred a spirit of independence. Once again Real Dogs joined with Real Men. They stood guard on the docks as the Boston Tea Party set off what was to be the War of Independence.

A similar spirit stirred in Europe, and Marie Antoinette's casual remark "Let 'em eat quiche!" became a rallying cry for the French Revolution.

After the age of revolution the world began to move even faster.

In 1789 Ben Franklin's wife told him and his dog to go fly a kite, leading directly to electricity, television, and "Saturday Night Live."

In 1803 Thomas Jefferson purchased the Louisiana Territory from Napoleon, thus paving the way for the famous Louisiana coon hound.

In 1903 the age of flight began with the Wright brothers at Dog Run, North Carolina. (Spuriously identified by cat lovers and quiche-eaters as Kitty Hawk.)

The optimisim of the new century was shattered in 1914 by World War I. The aftermath eventually led the west into the Great Depression. The country was finally rallied by Franklin Roosevelt and his dog Falla.

Soon the hopes for peace and prosperity were again set back, first by the hot war with Adolf Hitler and then by the cold war with the Soviet Union. In 1960 the Berlin Wall was erected. Shortly thereafter a Real Dog raised his leg against it.

The sixties brought a mixed bag—the Cuban missile crisis, flower children, Vietnam, and the Rolling Stones.

In this tumultuous period Betty Friedan traded in her Pekinese for a Doberman pinscher.

In the seventies a reaction to the social upheavals of the sixties set in and the "me" generation took over. The world was overrun by simpering, styrofoam lap dogs, and everyone started eating quiche.

Today, civilization is in crisis, and the perilous state of the Real Dog in this fractured world is a symptom of the general malaise.

While we need Rin-Tin-Tin and Lassie to show us the way, we're stuck with the likes of Benji and Garfield as popular heroes.

The problem isn't, as so many doomsayers whine, that this country is "going to the dogs." It's just going to the *wrong* dogs.

Real Dog Quiz #3

Q. How many Real Dogs does it take to polish off a case of Gravy Train?

A. Two. One to dig a hole and one to push it in.

6. Great Dates and Black

Great Dates

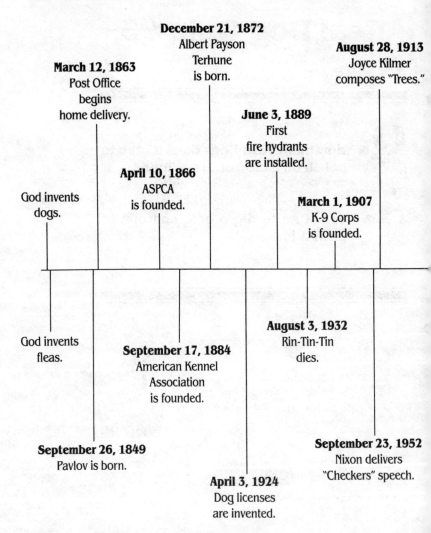

December 21, 1872
Albert Payson
Terhune
is born.

March 12, 1863
Post Office
begins
home delivery.

August 28, 1913
Joyce Kilmer
composes "Trees."

June 3, 1889
First
fire hydrants
are installed.

April 10, 1866
ASPCA
is founded.

God invents
dogs.

March 1, 1907
K-9 Corps
is founded.

God invents
fleas.

September 17, 1884
American Kennel
Association
is founded.

August 3, 1932
Rin-Tin-Tin
dies.

September 26, 1849
Pavlov is born.

April 3, 1924
Dog licenses
are invented.

September 23, 1952
Nixon delivers
"Checkers" speech.

Black Dates

Dates in Real Dog History

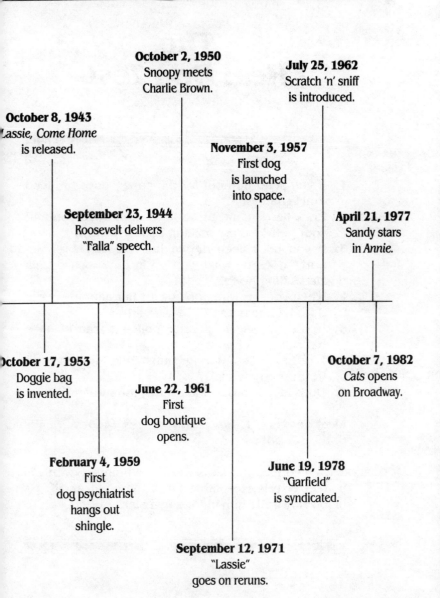

October 8, 1943
Lassie, Come Home
is released.

October 2, 1950
Snoopy meets
Charlie Brown.

July 25, 1962
Scratch 'n' sniff
is introduced.

November 3, 1957
First dog
is launched
into space.

September 23, 1944
Roosevelt delivers
"Falla" speech.

April 21, 1977
Sandy stars
in *Annie*.

October 17, 1953
Doggie bag
is invented.

June 22, 1961
First
dog boutique
opens.

October 7, 1982
Cats opens
on Broadway.

February 4, 1959
First
dog psychiatrist
hangs out
shingle.

June 19, 1978
"Garfield"
is syndicated.

September 12, 1971
"Lassie"
goes on reruns.

7

*The
Real Dog Test*

1. If you send him out for the paper, does he need exact change?
2. Does he demand to go for a walk while you and your girlfriend are making home movies?
3. If you fall asleep during the "McNeil/Lehrer Report," does he wake you up in time for *Godzilla Meets King Kong?*
4. When your ex-wife pops by for her alimony check does he bite her?
5. If you live in an elevator building, can he take himself out for a walk?
6. If he has to "go" during "Gunsmoke," does he wait for the commercials?
7. Does he use a Cinzano ashtray for a water dish?

Ideal Answers: 1. *No* 2. *No* 3. *Yes* 4. *Yes* 5. *Yes* 6. *Yes* 7. *No*

Each correct answer is worth ten points. Seventy is perfect, sixty is acceptable, fifty is marginal, and if he's below fifty trade him in for a hamster.

8

*Real Dogs
of Famous People*

*I*t's been universally noted that couples grow to resemble one another. This is as true for people and their dogs as it is for men and wives. (Cases where husband, wife, *and* dog become indistinguishable are not unknown, but are more in the realm of the occult.)

Although the most obvious manifestations of this symbiosis are physical, the most startling are in terms of character.

We've all seen the mincing quiche-eater waltzing down the street with his seemingly boneless Lhasa apso; the leather freak parading that freshly simonized Doberman with two sets of teeth; the neighborhood Yenta with her perenially kvetching Pekinese stuffed in a public television tote bag.

On the following pages we offer a few equally compelling, but ordinarily less accessible, examples.

DESCARTE'S DOG

At last! The perfect smile!

FREUD'S DOG

EINSTEIN'S DOG

HOWARD COSELL'S DOG

ALAN ALDA'S DOG

I recognize that our differences are long term and deeply rooted. However, I believe a mutually acceptable accommodation could be achieved if we were both willing to talk about it.

HELEN GURLEY BROWN'S
DOG

RONALD REAGAN'S DOG

He practically named himself. I call him Spot.

9

*Naming
the Real Dog*

Real Dogs, of course, name themselves. If you are patient and your dog is in the mood, he may tell you what his name is. (This is why there are so many dogs named Ralph.) Failing that, and assuming you don't want to call him "Hey, you!" you will have to name him yourself.

Here are a few basic rules:

Real Dogs are not named after celebrities, comic strips, sports cars, signs of the zodiac, flowers, imported cheeses, Baskin-Robbins's flavor of the month, or dead relatives.

Real Dogs' names are never hyphenated.

Real Dogs are never "so-and-so" the second, third, or fourth. Each Real Dog is unique.

Cute or comic names are definite no-nos. Dogs with names like Chow Hound or Dog-less MacArthur develop severe personality disorders.

Bear in mind that the best names are monosyllabic—Sport, Dot, Duke, Trish, Lad, Sarge, Boss, etc.

Two syllables, Rusty, Queenie, Terry, Maybelle, and Buster, are okay, too.

Anything with three syllables should be avoided and people who saddle dogs with names like Throckmorton should be locked in a dungeon with nothing but *101 Things to Do with a Dead Cat* for entertainment.

If you are dealing with more than one dog, don't succumb to the temptation to name them as a pair. Dogs named Dow and Jones, Step and Fetchit, or Mutt and Jeff end up destroying the furniture and biting people.

To sum up, try to see it from the dog's point of view. You wouldn't want to be called Highland Chauncey or Rough Weather Bluebell the third, would you?

10

*Sex and
the Real Dog*

lthough today's Real Dog is not unaware of the
sexual revolution, his amorous life hasn't
changed much since the late Mesozoic. In fact,
very little could be changed for the better. Oh, sure,
there's something about a leather collar with brass
studs that's a real turn-on, and sharing a Big Mac with
your date beats splitting a lemur femur. But the things
that really make sex good—tenderness, passion,
shared intimacy—have always been hallmarks of the
Real Dog.

Physical attraction is important, of course, but for
Real Dogs personality, intelligence, and a lively interest in current affairs count, too.

Real Dogs can show affection without ostentation. A
stroll in the moonlight, a stop at a drive-in movie, a
bone shared in front of a blazing fire. And if a romantic
evening stretches to dawn, a Real Dog always has
something yummy on the premises as an eye-opener.

Real Dogs are secure enough not to feel threatened
by an aggressive partner. They just relax and enjoy it.

Here are a few other notes on Real Dog sex.

Real Dogs don't worry about the G Spot. They've been hitting the bull's eye for millennia.

When Real Dogs stand stud it's *only* with a consenting partner.

Real Dogs don't confuse sex and exercise. There may be 150 positions in the *Kama Sutra,* but for Real Dogs, the old ways are the best.

Real Dogs are discrete; they never talk about it afterwards.

Real Dogs *like* doggie odors.

Real Dogs don't need computer-dating services, pornography, or Masters and Johnson.

Real Dogs don't ask afterwards if it was good. It's *always* good.

11

*The Real Dog
Library*

Dogs of War
A Hole Is to Dig
The Postman Always Rings Twice
Over the River and Through the Woods
Portrait of the Artist as a Young Dog
Jaws
A Tree Grows in Brooklyn
P.S. Your Cat Is Dead

12

How to Be Your Own Best Friend's Best Friend

Today, Real Dogs are an endangered species. The qualities that make them unique are being bred out of them the way taste is being bred out of tomatoes—in the name of convenience and added shelf life.

They are surrounded by wimpy-simpy cousins, raised and trained to accessorize the swollen egos of today's "me" generation. Their sense of self-worth is breaking down.

Real Dogs want to share, but how can you share with someone whose idea of a hot date is an evening with Pac-Man?

Real Dogs crave intimacy, but how can they get close to anyone whose idea of a fulfilling relationship is a weekly tryst with a Nautilus machine?

Real Dogs yen for life's simple pleasures—a cozy fireside and a spin in the back of a pickup truck through a brisk, autumn afternoon. Yet today they are asked to make do with the lifeless glow of a VCR, or to enjoy a midtown traffic jam in the back seat of a Toyota Corolla.

Clearly this won't do!

Bear in mind that every dog, regardless of size, breed, or place of national origin, has the potential to be a Real Dog. To help him, or her, on the road back, here are a few basic approaches.

1. Spend more time together.

This means just the two of you. Dogs like a party as much as anyone, but the key to restoring their sense of self is developing a deep one-on-one relationship. The occasion doesn't matter. A quiet evening in front of the refrigerator, a trip to the deli, Sunday morning sharing the paper. (And would it really hurt to bury a bone together now and then?)

There are endless possibilities, but the important point is that whatever you do, you do it together.

2. Share your feelings.

Real Dogs are naturally confiding but today, when everyone is scribbling a *roman à clef,* they have become wary. To get your dog to open up to you, you must open up to him.

We're not talking about office gossip or a recap of the six o'clock news. Learn to speak candidly and without embarrassment about your most intimate feelings. Real Dogs are the world's best audience. Soon your dog will be swapping confidence for confidence and you will have established the basis for a continuing and mutually enriching dialogue.*

3. Become a role model.

In a better world, your dog would learn the fine points of Real Dog behavior from another Real Dog. Since these are in tragically short supply, it may be necessary for you to do the job yourself. Granted, this is a bit tricky, but not impossible. And as a dividend you will find that in setting a good example for your dog, you will become a better, more interesting person yourself.

------

*NOTE: Real Dogs often lie down and shut their eyes while they listen. Don't be put off by this. It's just their way of concentrating on what you have to say.

Here is the basic Real Dog profile:

A *dignified bearing*

Real Dogs are well groomed, stand up straight, and have good posture. Your wardrobe should be conservative but relaxed. Not glitzy, but not preppie either. Shower regularly and avoid designer roughwear, penny loafers, and anything with someone else's name on it.

A *relaxed and confident manner*

Real Dogs are composed but not indifferent. If you can't watch William Buckley without foaming at the mouth, switch to Merv Griffin. Set a good example by being firm with doormen, cab drivers, and head waiters. Remember, Real Dogs were the first ones to decide that getting even is better than getting mad.

A *warm, nurturing personality*

Real Dogs are sensitive and caring, but not possessive. Be aware of the special occasions in his life. Birthdays, of course; all the national holidays, and remember that Arbor Day has a particular significance. Little treats from the deli counter are always welcome and an occasional rose by his dinner bowl is a thoughtful touch.

Finally, remember that physical well-being is as important as emotional health.

Encourage good habits in your dog by eating judiciously and taking regular, moderate exercise. (If you must have a pepperoni and anchovy pizza, eat it in the cab or at a friend's house.)

The above guidelines, followed in a conscientious and loving spirit, are guaranteed to lead your dog back to spiritual health.

Should you waver, bear in mind that a man never stands so tall as when he stoops to help a dog.

13

*Real Dog
Humor*

*I*f there is one thing that distinguishes Real Dogs
from their wimpy-simpy cousins, it's their sense of
humor.

Next to a good bone, there's nothing they enjoy
more than a good laugh.*

But remember that a sense of humor is a very
personal thing. The best jokes always touch our deep-
est concerns.

On Sundays, does your dog turn to "The News of the
Week in Review" *before* the comic pages?

If you're watching "Benny Hill," does he switch to
"Mr. Roger's Neighborhood" when you step into the
kitchen for a beer?

What is your dog getting night after night? One-
liners about Reagan's hairdo, Liz Taylor's waistline,

---

*Cats, by contrast, are notorious for their lack of humor. As a case
in point, Lewis Carroll's creation, the Cheshire Cat, became famous
for first cracking a smile.

Tiny Tim's ukulele, Frank Sinatra's ego, and George Steinbrenner's mouth. (And is there really anything funny about Rodney Dangerfield's failure to get respect?)

Perhaps your dog needs something closer to his own world.

The following rib ticklers have been especially chosen with your dog in mind by a blue ribbon panel of Real Dog humorists, and are guaranteed to return a smile to the lips of even the most lugubrious pooch.

I heard of Doggie Heaven, but no one ever mentioned Doggie Hell.

BARK
WORSE
THAN
BITE

According to your resume, you are paper trained, but not house broken.

Let me say this. I still have my teeth and if elected, I will not hesitate to bite.

The McCallister file, Chief! Somebody buried it in the backyard by mistake.

They kept telling me I was a good dog and,
apparently, I was.

14

Is Your Dog Real? Seven Danger Signals and What to Do About Them

1. *Does he eat sitting down?*

Real Dogs approach a meal the way Pete Rose approaches home plate: with enthusiasm and a determination to get their licks. Your dog's stance reflects his eagerness to "plunge right in."

Sitting down implies reluctance if not downright indifference. This may be the result of poor food choice. Check the label. If by-products and cereal total more than 30 percent, your dog is in danger of developing rickets. Anything over 40 percent would make Godzilla gag. Switch to 100 percent fresh ground chuck for seven days.

If that doesn't do it, buy a cattle prod.

2. *Does he fall asleep watching "Lassie"?*

We all have times when our personal lives are so exhausting we could sleep through a performance of Beethoven's "Wellington's Victory" in quadrophonic sound. Those bags under your dog's eyes may signify nothing more than an intensive love life.

Try not to be jealous.

3. Does he like to dress up in your clothes?

The lines between male and female have been blurring ever since they marketed the first unisex jumpsuit. The distinction between man and dog has been smudged since soldiers started wearing dog tags and dogs went into police work.

If this aberration can be limited to a rainy day diversion, and assuming he hangs your things up neatly afterward, there is little harm in it.

However, if he attempts to extend it to smoking your cigars and double dating, come down hard.

4. Does he prefer using a litter box?

This is peculiarly an urban problem.

The Real Dog's natural environment is the open countryside. Being flexible, he has adapted, more or less, to city life, but relieving himself in the street, in full public view, is still as embarrassing to him as following through with the pooper-scooper is to you.

At any rate, you should still go through the ceremony of walking him, so at least he won't be the laughing stock of all the other dogs in the neighborhood.

5. Does he insist on riding in the front seat?

For a Real Dog, a ride in the back of a pickup truck is the only acceptable excuse for the internal combustion engine. The next best thing is riding in the back seat with his nose sticking out the window.

Wanting to sit in front next to you bespeaks a sense of insecurity and/or mistrust. Perhaps you have inadvertently triggered it.

Do you try to drive and read a map at the same time?

Do you brake for animals?

Reassure him. Remember, the key to his behavior is your behavior.

On the other hand, he may just want to sit in your lap and steer.

6. *Does he need a night light?*

Cats are nocturnal. They really don't enjoy human company. The world for them is a better place when men are asleep.

Dogs, except for an occasional late date, tend to follow our patterns of sleeping and waking. Even so, Real Dogs are not afraid of the dark. If yours is, perhaps his eyes are going. Is he getting enough carotene and Vitamin A? Perhaps he needs contacts. (Actually, Real Dogs prefer aviator shades.)

Bearing in mind the Real Dog's exquisite sensitivity, another possibility comes to mind. Perhaps he thinks *you* need a night light and are too proud to admit it. Do you?

7. *Does he have a cat for a friend?*

We've all seen those photos in the *National Enquirer* of dogs nuzzling up to cats, chickens, hamsters, cockatoos, and gerbils. Don't you believe it!

Either the dog was sedated, or the other animals were stuffed.

Real Dogs are gregarious, but they select their friends with taste. If you see your dog getting cozy with a cat, his emotional situation is desperate and immediate action is called for.

Obviously, such aberrant behavior is his attempt to tell you that he feels you're drifting apart and that he's no longer sure of your affection.

In any case, professional intervention is called for.

Check your employer's group medial plan.

15

*The Real Dog
Hit Parade*

You Ain't Nothin' but a Hound Dog
Save the Bones for Henry Jones
How Much Is That Doggie in the Window?
Jingle Bells (sung by the Singing Dogs)
Digga Digga Do
I Found My Thrill on Blueberry Hill
Doing What Comes Naturally
How High the Moon
C'est Si Bone
Anything by Three Dog Night
Puppy Love

16

Living with the Real Dog

Although dogs are social creatures, they, like ourselves, need time alone. Ideally, a separate dwelling should be provided. For the city dweller, this is usually not practical. In that case, it is extremely important that the Real Dog have his own space. A special place never used for anything else.

Real Dogs don't demand luxury, but certain basics should be provided: a good blanket made of natural fibers (real dogs hate polyester), a generous water bowl, and something to chew on while reflecting on the events of the day. Since Real Dogs value their independence, a separate entrance is recommended.

Remember, a man's home may be his castle, but without a Real Dog, it's just a roof over his head.

17. Dog House

18. Dog House

19

Five Things You Won't Find in a Real Dog's Stomach

1. Tofu burgers
2. Alka-Seltzer
3. Adolph's Meat Tenderizer
4. Scope
5. Quiche

Real Dog Quiz #4

Q. How often should a Real Dog have shots?

A. It depends on how he holds his liquor.

20

*The Real Dog's
Wardrobe*

*T*he Real Dog's wardrobe is the essence of sim-
plicity. It starts with a genuine leather collar
(with or without studs). For the convenience of
friends who would like to keep in touch, a simple
nameplate with address and phone number is acceptable.

You will *never* find in a Real Dog's wardrobe the
following:

> rain boots
> a miniature, strap-on umbrella
> a Tartan jacket (especially
>   with a designer label on it)
> a rhinestone collar
> nail clippers
> mittens, earmuffs
> scarves or bow ties

Clothes may make the man, but the Real Dog pre-
fers to let it all hang out.

Hey, buster! Your fly's open.

Real Dog Quiz #5

Q. What does a Real Dog call a vet?

A. A former member of the K-9 Corps.

21

*Portraits
of Real Dogs
by Famous Artists*

No one knows what the masters who decorated the Lascaux caves had in mind. Were they summoning up the spirits of those great beasts, or merely attempting to brighten up a decidedly gloomy space?

One thing is certain, however. Man's desire to portray himself dates back to that moment when one of those artists decided to add his handprint to the murals of bison and deer.

Ever since then, the artist has really pursued only one subject—himself.

For the painter, the model has always been a kind of mirror.

On the following pages some great artists set out to immortalize their dogs and once again produce a portfolio of self-portraits.

VINCENT VAN GOGH'S DOG

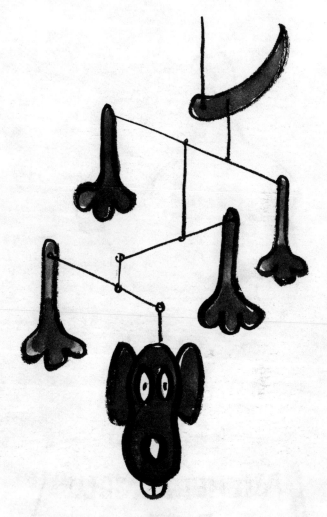

ALEXANDER CALDER'S
DOG

EDVARD MUNCH'S DOG

MARCEL DUCHAMP'S
DOG

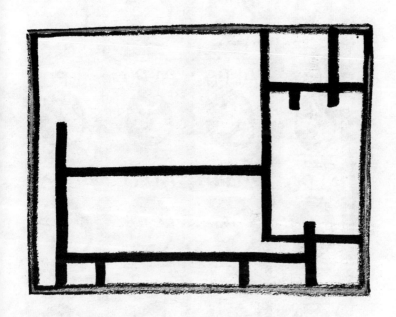

MONDRIAN'S DOG

ANDY WARHOL'S DOG

SALVADOR DALI'S DOG

ROY LICHTENSTEIN'S
DOG

CHRISTO'S DOG

22

*Great
Real Dog Quotes*

"Run, Spot, run." —Dick and Jane

"Mush, you huskies!" —Sergeant Preston of the
Yukon

"T'aint a fit night out for man nor beast."
—W. C. Fields, *The Fatal Glass of Beer*

"Come home, Lassie!" —*Lassie, Come Home*

"What have you got there, Asta?" —William
Powell, *The Thin Man*

"Good Lord, Holmes! It's the footprint of a
gigantic hound!" —Nigel Bruce to Basil
Rathbone, *The Hound of the Baskervilles*

"Which one of you bitches is my mother?"
—*Lace*, by Shirley Conran

"Arf!" —Sandy in *Annie*